AF810167

COMMUNICATION

Meta Strategies

Dharmendra Singh

GAURAV BOOK CENTRE PVT LTD
DELHI

Publisher
GAURAV BOOK CENTRE PVT LTD
4832/24,Prahlad Lane,S-207 Ansari
Road, Daryaganj,Delhi-110002
Ph.: 43570976, 23278261
Email: gauravbookcentre@gmail.com

Edition: 2014

© Author

ISBN: 978-93-83316-02-1

Laser Typesetting
JEE-VEE Graphics, Delhi

Price: 295.00

Printed
Vikas Computers, Delhi

Dedicated
To
My Guru
Charu Sheel Singh Ji

PREFACE

Communication which connects the societies and removes the sense of differences (dominant and dependency, superior and inferior, have and have not, big and small, rich and poor, north north and south south and so on.) and bring them at common place where all the gaps (social, political, culture, educational economic and others) become meaningless. It is participation where there is no place for occidents and orients, sanskritization (Brahmanism and untouchable) castism and communalism, regionalism and others because it believes in A.H. Maslow's. Self Relient and Being Needs, Nor-Thrope Fry's High Mimetic, Buddha's Nirvana, Mira's Love, Kabir's Nirankara Brahma and Gandhi's Non-Violence.

As a researcher, when we study the theoris of communcation, we find that all the components of communication, directly or indirectly have been under the control of authority who used it for their own vested intrests. And this picture can be seen from pre-civilization to civilization, modern to past-modern-era.

Theories which are borne out from these period for a moment, they tried to solve the problem of their predersors theorists thought but later on they failed and followed the same path which was followed ealier by other at that time.

This book is collection of research papers which are presented in national seminar at different parts of country and some are published in national journals which thought that these should assemble and published in a form of book. It has five research papers which are critically examined and detailed in the light of Indian thoughts as well as Western.

Whereas first chapter is concorned, its title is Inroads To Self: Creation Cocktail is an epic poem composed by eminent theorist poet, thinker and educationist, Dr. Charu Sheel Singh in which some suggestions and methods are given by him through which are communication can cross the ocean & evils which are existing since the origin of humanity. Great saints and scholars opinion are given here to make communication meaningful. Communication is metaphor not simile.

Similarily other chapters are also critically examinal either Religious Content and Media, Media and Development, Right to Information Act 2005 or Theories of Communication, all are detailed and tried to give solution which is already exist in Indian tradition's the Great Texts.

I am grateful to Dr. Charu Sheel Singh, Professor, Department of English and European Languages, Mahatma Gandhi Kashi Vidyapith, University, Varanasi far encoureging me to study the socialogy and anthropology of communication theories, for shaping my mind and soul to understand the basic concept of communication and its components in an sich form. I am grateful to Dr. Bishwajit Das, Director, Centre for Culture and Media Governance, Jamia Media Islamia, Delhi, far him motivation not to stop writing and detailing every thing critically. The co-operation and motivation of professor, Hemant Joshi, IIMC Delhi, Dr. J.S. Yadav, Ex-Director IIMC, Delhi, Dr. Anand Pradhan, IIMC, Delhi, prefessor, C.P. Singh, Dean and Head, School of Journalism ad Mass Communication, GGSIP University Delhi, cannot forgotten. My mother has always on stood with me for every endravour that I have ever made in life. I own her much more than a sentence of greatfulness.

My institute's chairman, Dr. Picheshwar Gadde, Secretary Mrs. Sunita Gadde and Director Jyothi Budharaju's contribution cannot be kept a side. They have always been the source of inspiration to me. My collegue's role to complete this work, how I can forget. I am really grateful to all of you.

Ram Navami 2014
Delhi

Dr. Dharmendra Singh
Professor, Head, BJ(MC)
Lingaya's Lalita Devi
Institute of Management and Sciences,
Mandi, New Delhi-47

CONTENTS

Inroads to Self: Creation Cocktail and Meta Strategies of Communication

SYNOPSIS

The governing hypothesis of this paper is that creation is symulteneously communication. Communication is that which medium. The unity of the content and the medium. The poem has cosmic implications of meaning which are capable of generating different generic possibilities, linguistic discoourses and models of commuications. The first part of this paper shall look upon the background issues where the universe has created by God out of the five elements emerges in terms of fine characters who comsitute and discoustitute cyclic rhythems is linear, metaphorical and projective manner. Earth is such an element, sky is another. Fire and water carry on the argument while the air supplies the movement.

I, Dr. Dharmendra singh, belive that when these five elements are not put under any kind of restrictions and a second nature is not imposed upon them, there is a great deal of the possibility that the channels of communication remain open. However, then the problem of assinilative and repressive communications arises. The first part mainly talk of the issues underlined above.

The second part of the paper, with the help of a available scholarship in the field of mass media theory of communication, shall illustrate how the creation cocktail is structured and for a student of mass communication what is the sufficient of this paper.

The third part will make comparative, critical and evaluative judgements making generalizations where nicessary.

Creation Cocktail is an endless discovery and re-discovery of what has been created by God. This includes, man's rediscovery of himself which is always in the process and never acquires a fulfillment. Creation Cocktail itself is a master-trope of language, culture, sensibility and understanding. It has Puranic layers of meaning within meanings, structure within structures which endlessly go on destroying and recreating themselves. Consider the opening lines of the poem:

Petrified silence grew
into directional depths of
hemispheres percolating
the being of an empty space.
There is a point,
destiny at the centre,
call'd bindu that cuts across
the enveloping dark
of a weeping earth
who is a woman too
waiting to be a mother.

Human body is an imposition of upon the human soul, however, natural it might be. The moment of dissolution of the universe carries a gap within itself that tries to fulfill its creative creation by creating another world. The hypothesis of this poem is that even though God endlessly circulates Himself through His own cosomocity into the direction depth still, the circulation has a mirror effect upon the created object.

Sancari Bhava as Bharat would say is basic to all of us but its realization in terms of degree and capacity is always a matter of difference. The five elements of nature constitute themselves in variety of ways and under the overall scheme of the things the constitution is nor exactly adequate to the original intention. This is what has created bricollage a rapture within thinking and expression, and stillness and so on. Communication always involves a certain process of empathy. Empathy is possible because all created objects are structured by the five elements. The empty space refers to the poem is the canvas, in the backdrop of which we have the enact roles and languages that makes us understand each others. The emptiness must be felt by all of us as human beings; it must generate a sense of anxiety which intern shall generate the need to communicate and understand each other. Emptiness also implies dissolution of differences which block communication at all levels. The point of Destiny in the poem found the destiny of being. The destiny is not intended here in the sense of fortune or astrology. It implies the existential character of the created world. Bindu is the potential source of thinking, becoming and being the basic seed- syllable of universe. Having established emptiness and Bindu as characters which are in the form of unmanifested universe, in its own rights, the poem introduces a character in flash and blood a woman who is actually the earth the material source of all manifest farms of production. However, the earth as woman is not satisfied with herself, therefore,, she s trying to be a mother. The earth as woman represents all working class people who are engaged in production but are deprived of their rights to manage its marketing. The earth as woman also represents alienation, segregation, disintegration, while the concept of mother is accommodative, inclusive and circulatory in each other. The basic agenda of the poem is between these two poles; the earth as woman and the earth as mother. The issue is that of such communication between the two that the earth as woman becomes the earth as mother. This also implies that the sender and the receiver are to be united at some level of the understanding or the other if communication has to take place ever the simile has to become a metaphor.

The content and the form of communication are issue of vital importance. The Bindu has generated Ram, Krishna, Buddha, Jesue among others who are the extremist point of the highest kind of idealism high mimetic of Nor-Thrope-Fry. All human societies have some ideal or the other to attain too; in other words all the forms of low mimeticism have got to transform themselves into high mimeticism. The process can begin in either of the ways from below or above. The Hindu theory of the incarnation of God is a tremendous marvel of communication. God is born as fish, bore the earth sustain itself upon the head of a snake. The dynamics of the circulatory power of communications can be more evident than this in the Indian tradition to reach the poem makes repeated references.

Beginning with the low mimetic which also has immanated from the Bindu and therefore has the power of the transformation implanted within it, the road to high mimeticism is wide open. The same potential power manifest itself in poet mystic of the Indian medieval era all of whom belong to the low caste but who carried the sublime (grand style) in high mimetic within themselves (Kabir, Raidas, Dadu, Tukaram, Chaitnya Maha Prabhu among others). The conceptual framework of role's actor which Krishna Himself in acted points to another form of communication and transformation. Krishna has given the concept of Lila which is a displacement of self interest in other that others might benefit. The basis meta strategy of communication is the loss of self interest in favour of the continuity of work that will benefit others.

The very idea of the Cocktail implies a mixture of discourses from different social groups. Creation is happening every moment just as discourses are being created every moment. It is on going activity. The idea is that in a colonizer, colonized relationship, the colonized is looked down upon disintegrated, segregated because the colonizer has his own self interest to flourish. In the context of poem, the fragmented section of human society, cannot say that they do not want to be sublime; sublime is not an option, it is a necessity the essential character of the Bindu. The modes of irony, satire, humour, pathos to which low mimetic belong, become integrated into the modes of analogical and anagogic imagination. It is the one which is circulated into the many because it was originally the one who had become many. The Sancari Bhava cannot function better than this. The charge of linguistic imperialism can be sustained because the cocktail is all in compassing and is mend for everybody to share.

The numerological symbolism in the poem tries to establish that communication is trans generic, trans worldly, trans continental, trans zonal, interpenetrating the manifest and unmanifest both. Five is the sense remote machine that we call the human body; seven symbolizes the seven lokas above the earth and the seven below it; nine symbolizes the nine hole of the human body, the nine fould lotus as it is called the Rigveda. The circulation of communication at all these levels is not possible unless the primary epistemological source (God, Hero, or Social Leader) is able to mystically assimilate the variety within himself as Bindu. The Bindu is the non-entity; only in that capacity can assimilate others. Therefore all executives, heads of states, scholars, teachers, social and political leaders have to renounce everything in the favour of the community of which they are claiming to be a representative.

The Pra-Bindu is beyond binary the invisible source of all visible creation, the unmoved mover of the universe as Aristotle called it, the still center of a perpetually rotating world as T.S. Eliot said or the constant as Hennery Bergson called it. This meta source of all forms of origination is a super magnet which assimilates as well as emanates anything imaginable. However there are other centers too, local, regional and zonal. These centers are situated at various levels of existence in the periphery which is outer space, apparently appearing to be full but in realty being empty. Because of their distance from the Pra-Bindu which is a meta center, these local centers develop various degrees of relationship as the lose touch with their own point of origination. Hence, the need for development of a diversity of discourses which, in term, require a cocktail to be intermoven as the story of a women who is all the time trying to be a mother. The tactical variety is dependent upon forms of structration which takes shape on the basis of economic, social and the religious interests of society.

All societies the world over witness a struggle berween the powerful and the powerless, the hegemonic and the marginalized and so on. Therefore, the endlessness of struggle for position and power through out history.

Creation Cocktail is a Mandela Poem and Mandela is always rotetave. As a result, the high and low shall continue to interchange their position in relation to a space which has remained always empty. It is not realy the cyclecity that involved here, it is movement at all levels of existence where nature is delivering its justice to each individual, each community and each nations. So in the end every body has to pass through an experience of gain and loss – which shall level all the distinction. All local centers in due course of time shall merge into the meta center while the meta center shall unleash new centers of distance and variations, differential degrees and uncommon velocities. Creation Cocktail therefore except the low mimetic as the fact of human existence which has the power to become a high mimetic on the basis of its regenerative capacities.

The speech of man
could not reach God
as man did not know
the language of the elements
which linked
destinies of corpuscules
in life-like-ness

In the western tradition the God has confused the speech of man at the Tower of Babel. In the Indian tradition silence is the better mode of communication because it evokes telepathic responses. The loss of communication is an effect of the original loss of the communication with man and God at the Garden of Eden. Creation Cocktail believes in Trans bodily communication which is available only when the language barriers are abolished. This is only for the good of man because its language carries differences and more so, makes them known to man. Because this situation is not going to arrive and because conception shall never become expression. Creation has to fail endlessly. Pralaya (dissolution) is another symbol of the same failure. For communication to take place, in any genuine sense of the term, we have to bring a mera-religion which judiciously distribute centers of power and has a willing capability to bind them together. This particular task is to be performed as much by nature as by man. Only a teleological relationship between the two shall form a new beginning.

Development and Media : Rhetoric and Reality

After the Second World War, the whole world had divided into two parts; capitalist and socialist blocks. America represented capitalism while Soviet Russia represented socialism. Their goals were different. One wanted the media should not be regulated by the state; it should have freedom and the free flow of information. The other had a socialistic point of view; it thought that media should not be free it should be under the control of the state. Thus America believed in the free flow of the information and liberal, free market discourse that championed the rights of media proprietors to sale whatever and wherever they wished. They believe that though the development of the world is possible through the free flow of the information. America thought the international communication was the key to the process of modernization and development for the third world. America gave birth to the concept of developmental media theory and international mass communication theory which could be used to spread the message of modernity. This would result in the transfer of the economic and the political model of the west to the newly independent countries of the south. The developmental theory firmly believes that it can remove traditional thinking in order to make the people equal on the basis of socio economic, political cultural, educational, psychological equality of opportunities.

Deniel Lerner, who was professor of political science at the Massachusetts Institute of Technology, was the exponent of this theory. His classical work in this field is The Passing of Traditional Society; Modernizing the Middle East (1958) in which he proposed that contact with the media helped the process of transition from a traditional to a modernized state. He characterized the mass media as a mobility multiplier which enables individuals to experience events in for-off- places, forcing them to reassess their traditional way of life. Exposure to the media Learner argued made traditional society less bound by traditions and made them aspire to a new and modern way of life. He thinks that the west's developmental path which improves the living conditions of societies is useful. It can remove the backwardness of the rest of the nations. His belief was that the western society had the most developed model of societal attributes (power, wealth, skills; rationality) and with the help of these thing; imbalance of the world mostly in the underdeveloped countries could be removed.

Learner's social development model consisted of the following components (S.R. Melkote and H.L. Steeves' communication for development in the third world page 114)

a. A core of mobile individuals whose psychological orientation made it easier to accept rapid changes in their personal lives and the overall social system.

b. An omnipotent mass media system that reinforced and accelerated societal and individual change by the disseminating the new ideas and thoughts and attitudes conducive to modernization, and

c. The corelation between the Important indices of urbanization literacy, media exposure and economic and political participation to establish a modern western type society.

Those countries which were colony of developed (North) countries till second world war, after it became indepent state, their socio economic conditions were measarable and this was not threating to its own rich people but also the rich of the rich countries (developed). That is why in 1949 US President Truemen made point four programme for the people of the third world countries which is the US would support the UN and help strengthen its ability to enforce its decisions. Second, the US would continue its work in revitalizing the world economy. Third, the US would "strengthen freedom-saving peoples around the world against the evil of aggression. Fourth, The US would embark on a new programme of modernization and capital investment".

Deniel Lerner, Wilbur Sehramm, Rogers and some others are motivated by the policy of Truman and moved toward the path of A.H. Maslow's which is known as Self-Actualization (A sense of self-fulfillment, deeper meaning in life's accomplishments; a sense of "happiness") which comes after the essential physiological requirement of food and shelter, the foundation of physical survival. Once those needs are met, concern of the second level can be considering the need for safety and security from the external threats. When the needs of first and second level are met, only then does Maslow see the human being as focusing on the happiness factors such as developing friendships, love relationships, and building up a sense of affiliation by being concern with social interaction. At that point the individual becomes concerned with self-esteem and gaining esteem from others. And finally, the self-actualization where, with the previous levels needs satisfied, a person experiences a need to reach full potential through maximum use of skill and abilities. This is A.H. Maslow's development (happiness, self-actualization). And all the modernization communications theorists directly or indirectly want to get it.

Another staunch follower of this theory is Wilbur Schramm. His well popular book is entitled Mass Media and National Development published in 1964 in which he prepared that mass media serves as a bridge to a wider world, a vehicle for transforming new ideas and models from the north (Developed) to the south (Underdeveloped, Developing) and within the south from urban to rural areas. But he feels that this one is not easy task as he says —"It takes a long time to modernize traditional agriculture not so much because the task is expensive as because it requires teaching new skills and new attitude and persuading cultivators to give up ancient practices and strongly held belief providing modern transportation, communication power and other social overhead tasks along time because it is very costly and requires a number of highly skilled worker and manager who are in short supply and must be trained. Education is slow not only because it is costly to train and pay techer bad build schools but also because education is by nature a slow process."

And he again says :

> "Where modern communication becomes so important to economic development. For the task of the mass media of information and the new media of education is to speed and ease the long, slow social transformation required for economic development and in particular to speed and smooth the task of mobilizing human resources behind the national effort."

It was the impact of the Schramm's book upon the United Nation which made them proclaims 1960's as the decade of development. In 1970 all the theorists of this field started this war for the development of society. The new approach was top-down approach to communications, a one way flow of information from the authority or the western developed agencies (with the help of mass media) to the southern, underdeveloped countries, without any feedback. They never asked whom they wanted to modernize and in what way. They also kept silent as to who would gain or lose. They denied any dimensions of development. In many southern countries, the income disparities increased over the succeeding forty years despite a growth in GNP.

We should not, however, forget that this development media theory has already improved the condition of the people a lot. The change of this theory creating local 'elites' is unfounded since there is no such intention implicit. It is another matter through those local elites does not want other to be equal to them. They had centered all the resources and did not go to disseminate. Thus, people in the underdeveloped countries think that earlier they were colonized by the west, now they have been colonized by their own race, casts and community's elites. Galtuing's is theary of Structural Imperialism in which the whole sociaty is divided two part core and periphery where core is so powerful which does not want that plriphery should come at that level where it is. This structure can he seen at every level, status strata of Indian sociaty.

Those people who have been repressed for centuries should not ask for their rights even the most primary once and that the other backward classes should not ask for reservations because it will infiltrate into those reservation if Brahmin and Kshatriya which have been in practices for centuries though without written character. Now it is clear to all that the trinity-politician, capitalists and media persons are united and always try to distribute the benefits of the society among them. They can be come close to be phrase of Parson and Paroto 'Circulation of Eletes. Politicians make rules which help capitalists and capitalists run media houses which helps politician to spread their vested interest content among the masses which helps the politicians to maintain their status quo.

Honourable V.P. Singh's Government passed Mandal Commission in 1990 to improve the living condition of poor section of Indian society which was very negatively presented by the Brahmin-Baniya oriented Indian media. What is highly understandable in this whole episode is the media has been able to create impressions that the posts filled through reservation are posts filled by incompatible people and posts filled without reservation are filled with competent people, the unwritten reservation notwithstanding. As analysis of requirements in center and states universities will show that the academic criteria has been the list consideration where as castes and another political factors have got a candidate selected.

The following practically example of central university will show the level of partiality and the violations of norms in practices, B.H.U. data, Banaras Hindu University Varanasi, Uttar Pradesh.

The media reports that reservation has been in practice for too long and the government should cancel now. The truth is that reservation posts have never been filled to their fault capacity, partly because of political reasons and practically the candidates are not available. A cursory glance at the overall of posts vacant in Indian universities. Otherwise mend for ST/SC and OBC, will make the position clear, lecturer in the department, on the cost of Dr. Jai Krishna, an internationally reputed scholar in geology. Academic achievement of Jai Krishna and M, Joshi is given below on other candidates V.K. Gairola's detail is also put here for comparison.

In this connection, it deserve mentioning that V.K. Gairola, at that time Head, was not only a known bootlicker of the V.C. but also a relative of M. Joshi through Murli Manohar Joshi the former H.R.D. Minsiter of N.D.A. (BJP Leader), The maternal uncle of the latter.

Bio-data of J. Krishna Vs M. Joshi & V. K Gairola

1. Number of Research Papers			
a. International	55	07	05
b. National	45	14	15
2. Cititation abroad abundant Rare None			
3. Teaching experiences			
a. PG	25 Years	30	05
b. UG	28	30	12
4. Independent Ph.D. Supervision			
	03	06	None
5. Fellowship & assignments abroad			
	15	00	00
6. Chairmanship conferences			
a. International	02	None	None
b. National	01	None	None

7. Invited Lectures abroad

25	None	None	

8. Membership of International Bodies

10	None	None	

9. Research Projects

a. International	05	None	None
b. National	05	None	02

Near about 35 pages detail are given by Dr. Subhash Rai in his book Clique formation and academic deterioration in Indian University (A case study of the Banaras Hindu University in 1998 which was publihsed by Radha Krishna publication Varanasi), B.H.U. where the picture of nepotism and castism could be seen which is indirectly exploiting the rights of others (Orientalist).

These orientlist or third world people's condition is prtray in the Myth of Development by O.De Rivero (2001) Page 63-64,

> "The country formerly known as the third world were always too politically, economically and culturally hetrogeneous to join forces as a world front based on common interest. Now, their interest are still more diverse and distant as the result of a greater differentiations in the levels of national misery among them. Divided into different groups, with greater of less poverty, the majority of this countries have not begun to compete in the prosperity rankings with the old aristocracy of industrialized countries. Instead they continue to compete among themselves for the world poverty ratings. This situation is major obstacle for true economic globlization. Since it prevents the majority of the world's populations from becoming consumers of products from the transnational enterprises. For the devotees of Adam Smith's The Wealth of Nations, ironically, the concern today seems to be the poverty of nations."

World's near about twenty developing countries population earn less than one dollar a day, means under poverty. Whereas India is concerned its eighty percent population earn twenty Rs. Per day which is disclosed by Arjun Sen Gupta committee's report which was set up by the government of India. One thing should be clear here if this much population is in this miserable position then this is not their own fault but the fault of the rulers of them who are governed by the mind-set of aristocracy. Who decides world wide where, what, how, and for whom to produce what. As it is written by Oswaldo De Rivero in his classic book The Myth of Development page no. 46 that- :

"Today the destiny of many national economies and cultures is being decided not in government offices or parliaments but in Internation financial markets of New York, Chicago, London, Singapore, Hongkong, Tokyo, Frankfurt or Paris, and in the board-rooms of the transnational corporations."

Development means neither Europeanizatton nor Westernization (Husserl) nor Brahminization/Sanskritization (M.N Srinivas). It is an on going process which can only have work at its centre for the peace and prosperity of all. One develops with in as well as without. The view of Gandhi was that development should begin from the grass root level of society. He wanted every individual to share the power that in turn helps people govern society.

Whereas media is concerned, since its origin it is doing its own jobs which is guided and decided by the gate keepers (Kurt Lewin) and the dream of Mcluhan's Global village is turn into reality. But whereas a benefit to it is concerned till date only chosen few are benefited and maximum are deprived.

From the first to the fourth five-year plans, the situation of development was quantitatively improving but qualitatively, the position of downtrodden was more or less static as it were. It was in 1970 that the scene of authoritarianism was changed to some extent. The demand for freedom and for selection led to the awareness of right and duties in the minds of the people. All spheres of society were going to be aware of the way development was to take place. It was the key role of modern media, which was improving the status of the people. People, (with the help of radio and newspapers) got adequate information, which was utilized for improving the lives of India. Women's education child education, eradication of poverty became prime agenda. Emphasis upon the use of technique in agricultural farming led to higher growth rate. Other programme about health, poverty, and unemployment were disseminated by the radio and newspapers alike.

But the whole mass media of India was being regulated with western theories of development. The theories were unfamiliar about the Indian landscape reality and the problems, people in India faced. However, western theories did much and were not mere utopia. The dominant culture of the west was followed by the upper castes of India. The development problems are everywhere the same. The difference is inequality. The Soviet Union Theory held good in Europe, even in India. The demand to break the monopoly of power groups is essential for change. The demand of Indian people to disseminate real picture of events and fulfillments of common minimum needs to more or less the same things as the surplus theory of the Marx, which implied distribution to the needy.

We see that among the people of India, there is a general awareness to participate in power. The monopoly groups, however allow this. The majority in India has been marginalized for long. India is known as a democratic country where every individual in supposed to get equal opportunities in education, employment etc.

There is a need for theory, which could change the ideology of the old periods. Indians need to approach a more humans approach without division and limitations. The concept of 'Brotherhood' is urgently requirement at present. There has always been difference between theory and practice more so in. India, which bounds in destination. Indians are divided by race, caste, community, religious fanaticism, feelings of the upper and the lower which are not bringing equality among segments of Indian society. We still need a theory, which could remove all these inequalities thereby silencing violence revenge etc. The literary play theory could do so. Play implies a negative capability to enter into others and understand their feelings, needs, emotions etc. This will instill kindness, pity for the poor. The innovation, which the law cannot bring, will then be brought. People will know that there is no difference between the character they lived for the time being and they themselves. When this will come in the time come in the field of communication, only then the goals and objectives will be achieved. We can explain the play with the help of the friends between Krishna and Sudama. Krishna rules over a Kingdom while Sudama is a downtrodden. The king Krishna asks Sudama to sit on his own thrown without any feeling of status. The paradigm should serve to bring equality in society. Another example, from Ramcharit Manas is when Lord Ram eats the fruits given by Sebery, a tribal woman. Rama is not status conscious there, there are so many other such instances in our religious texts, we need a will power to change over society on the basis of such paradigms. Lord Buddha's acceptance of Pali rather than Sanskrit reveals that one should transfer one's thoughts into the mass language. Sanskrit was the language of the haves while Pali was spoken by the have nots. Budha, without any complaint, accepted Pali because he knew the pain of the common people who were not allowed participation in the mainstream culture or power structure.

लोहे का स्वाद
उस लौहार से मत पूछो
बल्कि, उस घोड़े से पूछो
जिसके मुंह में लगाम है।

धुमिल

Bibliography

Ambedkar, B.R. Ghandhian; The Doom of the Untouchable, in Fred Dollmayr And G. N. Devy(eds) Between Tradition and Modernity, New Delhi; Sage Publication 1998.

Berelson, B. and Janowitz, M.: Social Control In News Room. In Wilbur Schramm(ed.) Mass Communication University of Illinois Press,1960

Carr,E.H.: The New Society, London:Mac Millan, 1951

Derrida,J.:Grammatology Motilal Banarasidass Publishers, Delhi 1994

Religious Content and Media : A Humanistic Approach

Religion and media both are very vast theme which will be tried to present few ideas, comments and questions which might help to future dialogue. A present T.V. has dominant position in comparison to other mediums of communication. Religion as a content, how is collected, selected and presented by it is a matter of discussion of this topic. Before going in depth it is important to know the meaning of religion. It has not single meaning but many. Some are presented here. As *Concise Oxford Dictionary defines* religion is human recognition of a superhuman controlling power and especially of a personal god or gods entitled to obedience and warship. Some others are interpretatively. As *William James* psychologist, has given it a psychological touch and defines that the religion is the feelings, acts and an experiences of individual man in their solitude, so for as they apprehend themselves to stand in relation to whatever they may consider the divine. 20th century sociologist, *Talcott Parson* defines the religion in the light of society and social set up as he says that it is a set of belief, practice and institutions which man have involved in various societies. Again religion is seen by some natural scientists eyes, one among them is *Solomon Reinach* who defines it is 'a body of scruples which impede the free exercise of our facilities'. And eminent literary man *Mathew Armold* sees it sympathetically and presents his view on it and says that it is 'ethics lightened, enkindled, lit up by feelings. *Herbert Spenar* says that it is the recognition that all things are manifestation of a power which transcend our knowledge or again humanity response to the divine.

Thus, religion is spoken of in a very broad sense, which includes feeling of transcendence, a cosmovision, an ethical evolution, an emotive element and a certain personal commitment.

SOCIETY AND MEDIA

After the second world war the scene of the whole world was changed. Ethnic society and its structure was broken and modern society became pluralistic society. The main reason of it was that several countries of Europe had opened their borders to inter the outsiders immigration who were different in every form and taste and they were mostly the eastern Europeans and Asians to fulfil the demands of their society and particularly in field of labour. It was plurality which had brought the innovative word at that time secularism. About that David Bosch rightly says, "one now distinguished carefully between 'secularism' which one rejected, and secularization which one welcomed and propagated.' In other words, the world has reached at certain point of autonomy-human beings have now come of age which affects the religious sphere. Thus the relationship with the Temple has become more critical more subjective and individuals.

In the modern society media are playing an important role to disseminate the information to the masses. The people those who are working in the media organization and are on the top position they say that all the event of society either man made or nature are covered by them and presented before the readers/audience. But some critics of media who say that 'value training' content are less covered in media. A well-known theologian used to say that we have to read the Bhagwat Gita, Vedas, Upanishads Ramayana, Mahabharat, Bible, Garanth Sahib and some other religions, holy text and the newspaper together.

But what newspaper which newspaper tell the truth, bring the information of what really happening in the world? Who dicides what will be the content of news? As we know that to open a big media organization there is a need of large amount, near about hundred crores rupees which can be invested only by the capitalist who wants to earn more than they he has invested.

So the meaning of ethics is not meaningful to him. All the private media organization offer a particular model of communication that will affect the content of it. Society and its elements which are *an sich*, real are not presented as it is but they are manipulated and interpreted by the gatekeepers of the media organization. Where as religions content is concerned it is also touched by them as the same way. In public service the supreme criterion is the presence of society and its institutions and respect for social, economic, political, cultural, education, environment and religions tradition too. In private service the objective is to reach the largest audience reader in order to obtain the greatest profit. What chance do we have of knowing ourselves and others. Problems, needs and dreams, if our voices and theirs are forced to pass thought filters that hold back all that affects the interests of the owners of the media? Today these filters/gatekeepers are minimum in their number but they have maximum powers. They are in dominant position regarding in the selection of the content of news and communication in our world/society.

Our audio-visual media's content are very trivious which attempt to excite our sense rather reduce it. Serious content, aesthetic standard and value oriented informations are like untouchable in the Brahmin/European mentality oriented media organization. The fragmentation of the image, of information, the manipulation involved in 'montage', creates a kind of partial 'truth' which prevents authentic communication.

And the result of it, those who are watching or reading them they have last their critical analytical power. The moment people lose this power, they are not able to communicate. They can only ape.

All the religions institutions are against of the media organization and reason is as they say that the religious contents are not collected, selected and presented before the masses *an sich* as Immanuel Kant says, noumenal or real. Those contents which are disseminated are interpreted and manipulated by gatekeepers of media organization which are phenomenal or which appears. Kant says that phenomenal is noumenal. The an sich world or noumanal world is perceived by an individual and presented before others which appears and called phenomenal. To present the *an sich* world there is a need of Sadhana, mediation through which grass body becomes the subtle body where all the different things become one, the reality, the noumenal, High mimetic of Nor-Thrope Fry. To obtain that situation only this path is appropriate. And those who want to go on the path of another trivious, low mimetic of Nor-thrope Fry, cannot reach to this destination reality. And that is why one devoted saint or mediator does not allow the media men to come and cover the spiritual content. They think they themselves are only suitable to teach that content to the masses because they are experts, not the media men. Only our spiritual experts, as they think, can protect loss of the faith of masses in the religious institutions.

Communication between the different groups of humanity was then so limited that for all practical purposes human being inhabited a series of different worlds. For the most people living in China, in India, in Arabia, in Parsia, were unaware of the others' existence. There was thus, inevitably, a multiplicity of local religions that were also local civilization.[1]

Today, the biggest criticism leveled by the people of religion is that media are usurping religious place in society. That is to give shape to a value system and to express the essence of a culture. For some people, for example, television has come to be a kind of religion. As if its secret role were to tell us how the world-ip, how it works and what its means. Therefore they think that the technological cosmovision offers at least three threats to religion. Firstly, it is derailing the greater part of interests, motivations, satisfactions and energies that are the purpose of religion. Religious people have feared the media especially because the media threaded traditional religious values and beliefs. They see how, as one result, one religious places are emptying. Secondly, religious language is being appropriated. New symbols images rituals and rites are being created. The mass media-especially television have taken command of the power of myth. One role of myth is to situate us, to define the world and our place in it. Thirdly, religious themes that have no connection with organized religion are being developed. This is welcomed by some independent evangelistic groups shaped by a remarkably uncritical faith in the media.

There are some people who are the critics of media, say that it does not and cannot present the truth before the reader/audience. Only fantasy and sensetionalization are covered and presented. Media have no relationship with realty and truth.

Malcom, M. a veteran English communicator, put his opinion about the medium which is an autonomous element capable of creating its own dynamic and, therefore, its own communication structure. Yet faith can be lived, received and shared outside society is structure and, so, the media are not only unnecessary but harmful. He again says that media as a "fourth temptation, which Jesus would have rejected because in reality this medium, because of its very nature, does not lend itself to constrictive purposes. On the contrary, media are giving to religious society something which is dangerously destructive.

There are some other critics who think to present the real content of religion there is a requirement of an environment. Some rules of behaviour are needed which are avoided by the present hyper informative mass media which present religious programme to watch. People eat or talk or distinct themselves with other activities and the way of behaving required by the religious celebration is lacking present, materialistic structure of our society has charged the way of living of people and that is why the expectation religious society is not fulfilled by them, it is lacking. And if we think that the television will get success only when it will present those content which are admired and watched by the people, the content would be obviously trivious not grand or lofty in manner and structure using.

Giorgio Giradet, an Italian Waldensian pastar, believes that one can final an alternative to extreme positions like the total rejection muggeridge. For him that alternative has to take five things into account:

(a) the importance of the media in a context that includes technical, financial, political and cultural aspect;

(b) that using an electronic medium, like it or not, is a political act;

(c) doing everything possible not to isolate the medium from reality;

(d) preventing technical questions from alienating the medium from reality (problems of quality, montage, etc);

(e) encouraging public participation, forestalling passivity.

He concludes: the struggle for and insistence on possible and sensible use of the media of mass communication centers in the end on reflection about the church. "We have to accept that in our world today mass media are more and more becoming the most important source of information and entertainment for us. We also need to recognize that they can play a significant role in encouraging participation in the search for a more just and peaceful world.

We live in a pluralist society in which the relationship of people to organized religion has been weakened. And yet spiritual needs appear more evident. Is it possible and desirable to us the media as new channels for manifestations of the spirit? No simple answer can be given to this question. Many different considerations have to be taken into account:

media ownership, legislations, professional rivalry, economic interests, social and cultural mores, the media as supermarket of religion, guideline for commercial advertising as a communication criterion and many more. What must not be forgotten is that communication is not offered to mass audience. People receive, select and interpret the messages sent to them from their own social and cultural viewpoints and, on the basis of that interpretation, draw their own conclusions. For this reason, a genuine encounter between media and religion carriers with it an attitude of respect for the dignity of people.

Reference

1. Beteille, Andre: Sociology, Oxford University Press, New Delhi, 2002.
2. John H. Hick: Philosophy of Religion, Prentics-Hall of India Pvt. Ltd., New Delhi, 2000, pp. 113.
3. Popper, Karl: The Open Society and Its Economic: Vol-2, Hegal and Marx, Routledge, 1945.
4. Singh, Dharmendra: Media And Mandal Adhyayan Publication 2005, New Delhi
5. Singh, Dharmendra: Mass Communcation and Social Development, Adhyayan Publication, 2004, New Delhi

Theoretical Corpus: Mass Communication Theories in the West and in India

Theories depict the socio-economic situation of particular times. As the time moves forward the changes within evolve' the newer genre of theories which answer to the social needs more accurately. Science and technology have not only changed the social system of world, they have-transformed the life style and behavior of the people at large. The culture and behavior of the primitive people is not required to be repeated today. There is no relevance of that system in the present day era of technology. We need a system that preserves good things of the old age. But the need is to combine them with new technologies available today. The industrial era set in because of the invention of electricity, which brings before us new norms and values and breaks the old spiritual ideologies. The pattern of understanding today has become more rational and scientific. The theory of communication, likewise, has evolved in its new shape due to the impact of our needy-oriented social life. The world is divided into many segments on the basis of socio-economic, political, cultural, spiritual, psychological and geographical, needs. Our communication theories for this reason are too many. They are developed on the basis of socio-economic and political situation of that particular nation or continent.

The following is on account of a few dominant theories in the Western canon.

AUTHORITARIANISM

Supposing modern communication came into the existence in 1450 under an authoritarian social set-up. In such a society, state is all powerful and the individuals have a secondary place. "The state ranks higher than the individual in the scale of social values."[1] Only under the state, the individual is granted progress and development. This means that the state not only ranks "the individual, but also that the state has caretaker function and the individual a dependent status."[2] The status of individuals, in authoritarian state differs but individuals are told to perform duties, which benefit the state. Under this concept the state is divided into two sects- the leader and those who follow the leader. The leaders are supposed to be divinely selected and they are naturally superior to others in terms of their intellect, wisdom and experience. The object of this state is to provide means to people to obtain their respective goals while following the rules and regulations of the state. The sources of authoritarians state originate in man assigning divine source to his will-to-power:

> It may be an accredited divine revelation, the wisdom of the race, or simply the superior ability of a leader or group to perceive dangers and opportunities. It may be, after a floundering reaction from disappointment with previously accepted truth, an emergent new promise-as sometimes happens when a country turns in desperation to a dictator. Always the source of truth has two characteristics: (1) It is restricted not every man has access to it. (2) It becomes the standard for all members of the society. To preserve unity of thought and action to maintain continuity of leadership, the authoritarian state employs all the tools of persuation and coercion it commonds.[3]

During the Renaissance, the authoritarian rulers like the *Tudors* and the Stuarts felt that they had divine right to rule others. These nobles protected their status in politics and war. They did not allow other to reach their position. Thus, politics and power became their sole property, which could not be shared. The state was secured only under their rule. This view was wide spread in society.

The same situation continued up to the *Middle Age* where the supremacy of Roman Church was completely established. This church spread the view that it had divine qualities and that it was established on the earth to rule over the human society. This church did not need give any freedom to those who did not subscribe to the church. The church and the state carried in full support to each other. The church, in that period, was the most powerful organization. No body could challenge conditions imposed by church upon the people.

The authoritarian state had accepted the political and philosophical background under which Plato wrote. Plato, however, argued that authority in the state could equally be divided. It can also degenerated.[4] He felt that the state could be secured only under the *Philosopher Kings*. The authoritarian were allowed to enforce this views no matter how wrong those views might have been. As Robert Maclver writes about the views of Plato.

> Plato wanted to 'co-ordinate' the life of the citizens under a strict cultural code that banned all modes of art and even of opinion not in accord with his own gospel. Very politely, in the *Republic,* he would 'send to another city' all offenders against the rigid rules prescribed for the artist and the philosopher and the poet. With equal politeness, in the *Laws,* he would require poets first to submit their works to the magistrates, who should decide whether they were good for the spiritual health of the citizens.[5]

The above-mentioned kinds are adopted in the early period of printing. The same view was put differently plots by different philosophers like George Hegel. Thomas Habbes and Machiavelli. All of them agreed that the highest duty of the individual is to be a member of the state. There is no freedom apart from the state. All the activity of individuals should be directed within the limits set by the state. The alone can provide security. So, the whole development and progress is obtained under the state. Thus, when print came into being and became a great voice, the government decided to check it. They controlled access by using patents or licences to printers and publishers, thus, assuming the power of determining who could enter the business. Since each licence 'had either a monopoly or a grant of vast privilege, publisher was quite likely to publish what his rulers wanted to publish. But late in the seventeenth century this kind of censorship was accepted because it was clums in appearance and laborious in reading. The cleaver journalists outwitted the censors. But later on, the government too, became conscious and familiar with the journalists activities. It decided to set forth clear guidelines for publication. It also ordered provisions for charging those who would not follow the guidelines. Thus, printing in its first two hundred years, was which chiefly another tool to promote unity and continuity within the state. Printing was to carry wisdom and truth as these were identified by the rulers.[6] The position of media at that time was that it could not but follow the authority. It was not expected that the media would criticize the authority or rulers. 'Discussion of political systems on broad principles was permitted; and it was often possible to criticize political machinery without fear of reprisal, but not the manipulators of the machinery.'[7]

To knowing the condition of communication in the realm of authoritarianism let us read the following:

> Stated negatively, there should be no publishing which in the opinion of the authorities, would injure the state and (consequently) its citizens. More positively, all publishing should contribute to the greatness of the beneficent state, which would as a consequence enable man to grow to his fullest usefulness and happiness. Significantly, one need not decide for himself, there is always an authority to serve as umpire. There is always revelation if one can know it the wisdom of the race or the past if one can perceive

it or the guidance of the leader - which is the easiest to perceive and the most common of guideposts in authoritarian society.[8]

In the last phase of the eighteenth century authoritarian communication took another turn. Its spirit, however, did not change. Those who believed in the democratic norms of communication still believed in the authoritarian supremacy. All underdeveloped areas and nations who were not aware of modern technology had to blindly accept. Conditions lay down by the modern developed countries. Under authoritarian, the information flowed from top to bottom. In this system, the model of communication is one where the communicator disseminates his views, thoughts, signs, and symbols unilaterally. The feedback was not thought to be necessary. It resulted in the authoritarian communicator not knowing the need of the people or the sentence. As it is known that 'a rule of thumb will suggest the vast spread of authoritarian communication; wherever a government operates in authoritarian fashion, an investigate is almost certain to find some authoritarian controls over public communication.[9]

At present, India's communication system functions under rules made by the Government of India. The rules are in favours of the freedom of the press. This fulfils the basic need of Indian citizens. However, in real practice the electronic/print media both are, more or less, controlled by the principle of authoritarianism. The selection of news, views, the circulation policy, management and all other things which are essential to the publication or broadcasting, are governed by the principle of authoritarianism. Broadcasting in India from another angle has become a state monopoly and in some of them the fact of an authoritarian relationship to government is dear even through the government itself cannot be described as authoritarian.[10]

In India, this authoritarian thought and principle was never taken and implemented as it was in its original form. The belief of Hegel, Hobbes and Machiavelli acquire a new shape. They thought that the whole development and prosperity could be possible only under the guidance of an authorial set-up. The leader of this system did not want to disseminate those things, which would lose them their authority. The authoritarian (ruling) class created its own rhetoric of exploitation. It transformed messages in a language whose sign and symbol the common people did not understand. The ruling class had a deliberate strategy of not educating the masses properly. The religious text called *Manusmiriti* by Manu as a glaring example of this whole society was divided into four *Varnas, Brahman, Kshtriya, Vaishya* and *Shudra.* Their duty and function was well defined under religious sanction. In theory, all the four *Varnas* should have united but in practice it never happened. The whole social set-up was broken and the *Varnas* failed to establish harmony. An ignorancy and lack of knowledge about customs, culture, rituals, code and conducts resulted in disaster for society. The first three *Varnas* enjoyed a good relationship among themselves but the Shudras were totally neglected. The communication among all *Varnas* was never harmoniously established. The Brahmanical thoughts were deliberately enforced upon others. Brahman did not accept the Shudras system. The communication was one sided and followed from top to bottom. It was never two-way communication. Thus, the whole society was controlled by levels of authoritarianism. Kautilya's *Aartha Shastra* too reveals aspects of the authoritarian principle. We may say that:

> From country to country, these categories often shift with the tides of politics. But the fact to clear that authoritarianism has been the dominant philosophy behind public communication for more year in more countries than has any other pattern of thought.[11]

Raja Ram Mohan Roy had to establish *'Brahma Samaj'*, Dayanand Saraswati established *'Arya Samaj'* while *Ram Krishna Mission* vowed to emancipate the barriers of caste, creed, religion in order to establish harmony in Indian society.

The social reformers fought against the hypocrises of Indian authoritarianism who themselves did not follow rules they laid for others.

LIBERTARIANISM

Every theory has its own seeds of destruction. Authoritarian theory vanished because of inherent defects. Authoritarianism flourished during the last of the fourteenth and the beginning of the fifteenth century. The rapid change in traditional views was brought by the development in science and technology. And this knowledge became the enemy of the traditional thought where leaders of authoritarianism told that they were the chosen few and had divine sanction to rule over the masses. Only under them, the society could be safe secure. This myth had been broken by the knowledge of science. The authority of Church and Kings were challenged and a new class came into being which now is known as the middle class. The capitalism also challenged the old idea of fixed status and ushered in a world of social mobility. There were political revolutions, like the one in England against the Stuarts, challenging the right to arbitrary rule.[12]

It was the Enlightenment movement, which started in the seventeenth or eighteenth centuries. It represented an intellectual change, which was one of the most revolutionary intellectual movements of all time. About its basic idea Cassirer said: "The conviction that human understanding is capable of its own power and without recourse to supernatural assistance, of comprehending the system of the world, and that this new way of understanding the world will lead to a new way of mastering it."[13]

All pre-suppositions had to pass the test of science. Superstitions, orthodoxies and authoritarians had no place under science. The world was realized to be round and man had looked at the planets through telescopes, the man of this period was declaring his independence from all outside restriction on his freedom. He used his understanding to solve religious, political and social problems.[14] Thus, in the 17th and 18th century rapid changes were taken place in all sphere of society-social political, philosophical, geographical, psychological among others. The result was that the people of authoritarian rule started to stand against such changes and a new theory called prenatal dislodge authoritarian theory. It was known as libertarian theory. The future and object of this theory were:

> The libertarian theory of communication grew with and from these revolutions of mind and spirit. Much of its doctrine and many of its fighting phrases were the thought of early philosophers. Descartes was one of the first, his sweeping influence deriving from his emphasis on reason on the road to truth. The most influential of the libertarian philosophers in England was John Locke who was pivotal in intellectual change. Arguing that the center of power was the will of the people, he held that the people delegate their authority to the government and can withdraw it any time.[15]

John Locke gives too much freedom to the masses who can accept or reject the power of authority because authority itself is the will of the masses. Locke's philosophy gives too much power to the individuals, which would have never allowed authoritarianism. We can notice the basic differences between the two from the following.

According to authoritarian theory, of course, man is a dependent creature, able to reach his highest level only under the guidance and care of the state. According to libertarian theory, he is independent and rational, able to choose between right and wrong, good and bad. In authoritarian theory, the state outranks the man on the scale of values. In libertarian theory the state exists only to provide a proper milieu in which man can develop his potentialities and enjoy a maximum of happiness. If the state fails in this mission, it can be radically changed or abolished.[16]

Thus, the liberatarian theory of communication except that the society would provide a free market for idea so that men may exercise reason and choice. This theory does not the formal control of the state. It chooses to trust the self-righting process of truth. This implies that idea must have an equal change and that everyone must have assess to the channels of communication.[17] Thus, this theory is in favour of the free market and private owned media. Anybody could become part of the process who would have sufficient capital to manage. The newspaper, magazine, and broadcasting, in other words, print media and electronic media, could be started by anyone who had the capacity and the capital to do so. And in this pattern at present, United States, United Kingdom, Europe and India, too, have a number of print and electronic media which privately owned.

There is also a dark side of the theory, which affects the developing countries the most. The share of the capital in the hands of the few in developing countries. These few could misuse their freedom by carrying none for their own status quo rather than uplifting the downtrodden. The money game comes to center upon power - status-capital. The capitalist class would not remove poverty for it was not serve its desired end of maintaining status quo. We are still far from a social welfare state. Capital, too differ from country to country. American capitalist cannot be put under the same class as Indian capitalists for this reason there are many gaps left in ushering the social cause of equality, liberty and fraternity.

At one place, there are highly developed countries like America, U.K., France and others. At another side, all developing countries are struggling to solve their problem of unemployment, poverty illiteracy etc. In such conditions the flow, in largely one sided from top to bottom. A general lack of technology and expertise in particular fields adds to the problems of developing countries. The developed countries disseminate only such information; news/views, which they feel, will benefit them. This results in a communication noise, which takes place due to lack of proper knowledge of signs symbols and about the production, which they present through the advertisement, customs and culture. The developed countries serve another version of the principle of authoritarianism. They want to disseminate only those things, which are useful to them. It does not matter what others need are. In reality the flow of information is one way from top to bottom.

The individual or poor countries are left with no power to speak against technological imperialism. The powerful communicator does not want mediation or sharing. The advocacy of two-way communication is not fulfilled. In India, Raja Ram Mohan Roy, Swami Dayanand Saraswati, Gopal Krishna Gokhale, Bal Gangadhar Tilak, Swami Vivekanand, Ambedkar, Jawahar Lal Nehru had to revolt against authoritarianism to get the liberty in socio-economic, political, cultural, educational fields and all the other spheres of the life of the people. It was the combined effort of the people, which was freedom her India and India became an independent country. It established its own communication.

SOVIET COMMUNIST THEORY

The seed of this theory was sown in the libertarian land when people got freedom to make their private property. This resulted in a transfer of land from the hands of state to that of the capitalist class. The whole economic control came to be exercised by a few who thought that they alone had the best of capacity to do good to society. Such rhetoric did not help alleviate poverty, which left no way for poor but to agitate. The resources of production were again centered in the hands of a few whose attitude was no different from those belonging to the authoritarian class. The exploitation and torture of the rest of people had become a routine. The social conditions had become worst because the whole socio-economic, political power was concentrated to few. The centralization, of these means of production compelled masses to revolt. The man who led such revolt was Karl Marx, a German exile, who constructed his general theory of history. His concept is based on dialectic of social change. Marx was indebted for his dialectic to Hegel. Marx adopts Hegal's dialectic and turns it upside down. He thinks-

Hegel, an idealist, "the idea," the life process of human brain, made the dialectic work. Marx held that for Hegel dialectics "is standing on its head. It must be turned right side up again, if you would discover the rational kernel within the mystic shell.[18]

According to Marx, the productive forces are greater than the class who' owns production capitalists. As he observed it,

> Capitalism contained the seed of its own destruction. It would always be riddle by economic crisis and depression. The rich would grow richer and fewer; the poor, poorer, more numerous and more desperate. The last stay of capitalism would be imperialism, which would breed wars and more misery. Finally the working class unable to contain their misery and frustration any longer, would rise, liquidate the surviving capitalist, take over the means of production, and then built a classless society. Since all society is economically determined, Marx said, the political system, the arts, religion, philosophy and all other components of culture would change with the economic system.[19]

Marx's approach is that through proper distribution of economy the inequality can be removed and the harmony restored in society.

Actually the philosophy of *Dialectical Materialism,* as formulated by Marx was based upon 'the common ownership of the means of production, or negatively the abolition of private property.[20] This private property, as it is mentioned above, came into being in the libertarian period which had spread in society imbalances and gaps. Marx wanted to emancipate suffering people from problems. He felt that when all the means of production will be commonly shared, much of the common suffering would disappear. "The basic goal of communism is the sharing, in common, of those material goods which are the means of production, particularly land and raw materials."[21] This clearly shows the attitude of Karl Marx. He is not in favour of any class or state. According to him, he expects not only a classless society but also stateless society. In the field of communication this would come to mean that Marx does not advocate any class or caste or government or society- based information. Because he knew that whenever these had disseminated information, it was based on the destination as to what benefited them and what not. Marx clearly knew that all polities of concentration of power and resources would never disseminate freely and equally. He feels that information should be based to educate the great mass of the workers and to organize them. The role of state is only to control class-conflict.

Karl Marx never gave any theory of communication. It was the Soviet leaders who deduced a theory of mass communication after Marx's assumption. By trial and error, and under the force of need, the Soviet theory of communication developed as an integral part of the Soviet state where it is said that the press should be a "collective propagandist, collective agitator-collective organizer."[22] It is generally believed that in the Soviet communication theory there is no place for criticism. It is not so. Lenin was in favour of not only criticism but self-criticism too, which alone could expose the drawbacks.

> One of the chief function of the press is to carry criticism from the top-especially from the party and from below from individuals, working collectives, or trade unions. But there is a sharp limitation. Soviet journalists may criticize people, including high bureaucrats, but no institutions. The foundations of Marxism. Leninism are sacrosanet. The *Praveda,* the central organ, often carries an article critics of factories, districts, or region which fail to meet produces quotas, and ministries and bureaucrats are attacked the failing to introduce new methods.[23]

This clearly removes our confusion whether Marxist theory can be criticized or not. The charge of authori tarianism is also laid against this theory. The following will make clear the differences between these two:

> The mass media under the old authoritarianism were and are largely privately owned, except in some countries in the case of broadcasting these media were and are controlled primarily by patents, licensing, guides, government pressure and censorship. Communist media are usually controlled by ownership, by party personnel in key positions, by directives, review, criticism, and censorship. The essential point is that in the order authoritarian system the media have typically been part of the business system and to that extent less exclusively an instrument of government. They have been in bondage to the state. The Soviet media are *in* and of the state.[24]

This is clear from the above that this theory gives so much importance to the common man than to society or state. Marx's approach is that freedom is for the people, not for the media. The problem is to get freedom from harmful information, debasing entertainment, false teaching-whose criteria shall be laid down by the leaders of the people from time to time. The goal is collective results classless society and the people's state. There is a continuing emphasis in Marx the good that the state and society should perform the welfare of the proleteriat.

According to the communist belief, the improvement of society security, must precede the development of man, and both' are dependent on the material welfare of society.

This theory emphasizes commoness and collectiveness. It keeps the holistic concept which is based on humanistic approach. And it declares that the welfare of society and the world is possible only when the proletariat is informed properly. But no doubt Karl Marx's dream remained a dream. It never took its real form because of the disintegration of society. Those who were haves did not keenly leave this property as Karl Marx expected. So the flow of information still remained in the hand of authoritarians.

Marx's philosophy is based on the dialecticism of Hegel which was spiritual. Marx took it to material ends. On that view he profounded his theory, through which he wanted to establish a proletariat society or generate proletariat communication system. In India, there were too many ideologies which were based on spiritual and social grounds. Raja Ram Mohan Roy breaks the tradition of Hindu rituals, child marriage, Sati on the view of *'Advaita'* and hopes that only on that basis, the Indian society could get its basic goal of development and progress. Like Marxism which revolts Brahmincal system is resulted against authority it implies capitalism. Another instance is of Swami Dayanad Saraswati who told the down-trodden (Sudras) to bear the sacred thread of Brahmin to unify them into the main stream of the Hinduism. There are so many examples, Buddha, Mahavir Swami the founder of Jainism, Guru Nanak, the founder of Sikh religion, all of whom spread equality so close to Marx.

SOCIAL RESPONSIBILITY THEORY

It is not easy to overcome the defects of authoritarian communication theory as it surfaced in some form or the other in any other kind of theory. The main object of libertarian was to decenter the power of state to the mass and give them proper environment to develop their personality. They succeeded too but the power earlier centered in an authoritarian state came to rest in some elites among libertarians. They also started to function much as authoritarian did. The same thing happened with the Soviet Theory where authoritarianism stood firmly. Only words, changed, the exploitation of the proletariat continued. All these theories, for a short time, achieved their goal but in long term, some evil entered which made theories function no better than authoritarianism. Only scientific development gave new words to old systems. Marx's communication theory needs change too.

"One of the basic needs of society is the Enlightenment seemed to be to free the press from the state so that it could operate as a check upon government and as a vehicle through which man might discern the truth. For more than half century now, however, the tendency has been to examine the performance of the press and perhaps to lay some requirements upon it that would be quite foreign to the spirit of libertarianism.[25]

The whole system of mass communication has really corrupted the masses. The distribution of information accordingly to the likes and dislikes of few can only lead to disconnect. Time and again, due to lack of proper dissemination of information there was communication noise.

The general themes of the criticism of all the media have been summarized by *Theodore Peterson:*

1. "The mass media have wielded enormous power for their own ends. The owners have propagated their own opinions, especially in politics and economics at the expense of opposing views.
2. The mass media have been subservient to big business and at time have let advertisers control editorial policy and editorial content.
3. The mass media have resisted social change.
4. The mass media have often given more attention to the superficial and the sensational in this coverage of human happenings than to the significant, and their entertainment has often lacked substance.
5. The mass media have endangered public morals.
6. The mass media have invaded the privacy of individuals without just cause.
7. The mass media are controlled by one socio-economic class loosely "thc business class" and access to the media is difficult for the new comer; therefore, the free and open market of ideas is endangered.[26]

Under these circumstances, the mass felt suffocated and restless. They started to think, there should be something different which could make editors responsible. The broadcasters of the world media should also share such responsibility. Thus, Social *Responsibility Theory* came into being about which John Merrill, has argued;

> This so-called "theory" of social responsibility has a good ring to "it and, like" love" and "motherhood" has an undeniable attraction for many. There is a trend throughout the world in this direction, which implies a suspicion of, and dissatisfaction with the libertarianism of Milton, Locke and even Jefferson. Implicit in this trend toward social responsibility is the argument that some group (obviously a governmental one, ultimately) can and must define or decide what is socially responsible. Also the implication is clear that publishers and jouranlists acting freely cannot determine what is socially responsible nearly as well as can some "outside" or "impartial" group. If this power elite decides the press is not responsible, not even the First Amendment will keep the publishers from losing this freedom to government. This would appear to many as a suggestion of increased power accumulation at the national level, a further restriction of a pluralistic society...
>
> Many persons will object to this line of analysis and will say that "social responsibility" of the press of a nation does not necessarily imply government control. The writer contends that ultimately it does, since it left to be defined by various publics or journalistic groups the term is quite relative and nebulous; and it is quite obvious that in the traditional context of American libertarianism no "solution" that would be widely agreed upon or enforced could ever be reached by non-government groups of individuals.[27]

The argument of Merrill is that social responsibility is defined by the journalistic groups and enforced not at all.

He said again if it were defined and enforced by government, it would be nothing more than an authoritarian system in disguise.[28]Thus, we see that every theory claim it is responsible towards the people. Even an authoritarian claims so, and do libertarians and Marxists. All theories function within limitation and, as such, never achieve their goods. If they did achieve this goals, communication noise would not have

The new social responsibility theory is also governed by the journalistic groups and they are responsible to society. However, there is guarantee whether they will succeed. They could also be authoritarians in a democratic dress.

> Under libertarianism, the media were exacted to reflect the world as their owners saw it, to tell the particular truth the owner preferred, to distort, to lie, to vilify, all with the confidence that rational men could discern truth among the flasehood. No one today has confidences in such belligerent libertarianism.[29]

The basic idea of all theories is to disseminate information to the mass through which they can achieve their developmental goals. They can know the policies of government participate in events-political and social as well as economic and cultural. All theories-authoritarianism, libertarianism, the Soviet theory and the social responsibility theory, differ only in their approach to the names and not in their intention. Theodore Peterson say that 'mass media always are controlled by one socio-economic class-the business, class and this class has published and broadcast only those things which they liked, they had never thought the demand and need of the mass. And that is why the mass of world lived under the condition of downtrodden. Where they had no choice to say to the gatekeepers of print/ electronic to send them as they wanted.[30] There generally, is one communication in practice. However, it is believed that the media should follow the norms of society but the outlines of these norms are not clear.

In spite of these four press theories, Mc Quail Denis introduced two other theories in 1983 in his book-entitled *Mass communication Theory.* The theories are *Development media Theory* and *Democratic Participant Media theory.* All theories are products of their particular times and period so the rapid change of time, and the highly developed technology has brought a new scene in the mind of the west. The west desired to inform the rest of the people about technology of which people were not aware. It is the firm belief of the western media that traditional societies can only be transformed by technology and science. Once the technology is in the hands of the people, they shall have access to power and function.

Actually all the four press theories did obtain their goals which were latent in their ideologies. The result was that the gap among people nations remained. The flow of information was already from top to bottom. There was no balance and that is why the countries, and the world as such was divided in two parts; one which had too many information and technology and the other which had nothing else except poverty, illiteracy unemployment and some other disasters. There was no healthy communication among them. The need was overcome these inequalities, which had spread among societies/nations. In 1981, the 21st General Conference Session of UNESCO, held in Belgrade, passed a resolution.

The resolution proposed:

(i) Elimination of the imbalance and inequalities which characterize the present situation;

(ii) Elimination of the negative effects of certain monopolists, public or private, and excessive concentrations;

(iii) Removal of the internal and external obstacles to a free flow and wider and better balanced dissemination of information and ideas;

(iv) Plurality of sources and channels of information;

(v) Freedom of the press and information;

(vi) The freedom of the journalists and all the professionals in the communication media, a freedom inseparable from responsibility;

(vii) The capacity of developing countries to achieve improvement of their own situation, notably by providing their own equipment, by training their personnel, by improving their infrastructure and by making their information and communication media suitable to their needs and aspiration;

(viii) The sincere will be developed countries to help them attain these objectives;

(ix) Respect for each people's cultural identity and for the rights of each nations to inform the world public about its interests, its aspiration and its social and cultural values;

(x) Respect for the right of all peoples to participate in international exchange of information on the basis of equality, justice and mutual benefits;

(xi) Respect for the right of the public of ethnic and social groups and of individuals to have access to information sources and to participate actively in the communication process."[31]

DEVELOPMENT THEORY

After the Second World War, the whole world had divided into two parts-capitalist and socialist blocks. America represented capitalism while Soviet Russia represented socialism. The goals were different. One wanted that the media should not be regulated by the State; it should have freedom and the flow of information. The other had a socialistic point of views; it thought that media should not be free, it should be under the control of the State. Thus, America believed in the free-flow of information and a liberal, free- market discourse that championed the rights of media proprietors to sell wherever and whatever they wished. They believed that through the development of the world is possible through the free- flow of information. American thought that international communication was the key to the process of modernization and development for the third - world. America gave birth to the concept of the developmental media theory and international mass-communication theory, which could be used to spread the message of modernity. This would result in the transfer of the economic and political models of the west to the newly independent countries of the south. The developmental theory firmly believes that it can remove traditional thinking in order to make the people equal on the basis of socio-economic, political cultural and educational equality of opportunities.

Deniel Lerner, who was professor of political science at the Massachusetts Institute of Technology, was the exponent of this theory. His classic work in the field of *The Passing of Traditional Society* (1958) in which he proposed that contact with the media helped the process of transition from a 'traditional' to a modernized state. He characterized the mass media as a 'mobility multiplier', which enables individuals to experience events in far-off places, forcing them to reassess their traditional way of life. Exposure to the media, Lerner argued, made traditional societies less bound by traditions and made them aspire to a new and modern way of life. He thinks that the west's developmental path is useful to remove the backwardness of the rest of the nations. His belief was that the western society had the most developed model of societal attributes (power, wealth, skill, rationality) and with the help of these things; imbalance of the world mostly in the underdeveloped countries could be removed.

Another staunch follower of this theory is Wilbur Schramm, who is known as a theorist of modernization. His well popular book is entitled *Mass Media And National Development* in 1964. He proposed that mass media services as a bridge to a wider world, a vehicle for transferring new ideas and models from the North (Developed) to the South (Underdeveloped, Developing) and within the south, from urban to rural areas. But he feels that this one is *not an* easy task. As he says :

It takes a long time to modernize traditional agriculture not so much because the task is expensive as because it requires teaching new skills and new attitudes, and persuading cultivators to give up ancient practices and strongly held beliefs. Providing modern transportation, communication power, and other social overhead takes a long time because it is very costly and requires a number of highly skilled workers and managers, who are in short supply and must be trained. Education is slow not only because it is costly to train and pay teachers and build schools, but also because education is by nature a slow process. As a French Word for education, *formation,* suggests, education aims at the formation of a new person, with new horizons, new skills, new goals. It does indeed take a long time. All the kinds of human change required for economic development take long, and are costly and difficult. And yet, as Millikan and Blackmer argue so possessively," the paramount requirement of change in any society is that the people themselves must change.

And he again says :

Where modern communication becomes so important to economic development. For the task of the mass media of information and the "new media" of education is to speed and ease the long, slow social transformation required for economic development, and, in particular to speed and smooth the task of mobilizing human resources behind the national effort.[32]

It was the impact of the Shramm's book upon the United Nation which made them proclaim 1960s as the *Decade of Development.* In 1970, all the theorists of this field started their work for the development of society. The new approach was top-down approach to communications, a one-way flow of information from the government or the Western developed agencies (with the help of mass media) to the Southern, underdeveloped countries, without any feedback. They never asked whom they wanted to modernize and in what way. They also kept silent as to who would gain or lose. They denied any discussion of the political, social or cultural dimensions of development. In many southern countries, the income disparities increased over the succeeding thirty-two years-despite a growth is GNP.

We should not, however, forget that this development media theory has already improved the condition of the people a lot. The charge of this theory creating local 'elites' is unfounded since there is no such intention implicit. It is another matter through that local elites do not want other to be equal to them. They had centered all the resources and did not want to disseminate. Thus, people in the underdeveloped countries think that earlier they were colonized by the west, now they have been colonized by their own race, caste and community's elites. However, this theory had given freedom to accept any mode of information and ideology, which might be of benefit to the people of any caste, creed, culture or religion.

DEMOCRATIC PARTICIPATION THEORY

The democratic participant media theory has its distinct place among the developmental theories. The voice arose against the developmental theory on the charge that it had one-way flow of information only, which is vertical from top to bottom. This creates imbalance in society and there is no harmony left among the people. Under this theory, whether, intended or not, the rich became richer and the poor, poorer. Under such condition the flow of information does not find its own goal. The non-grasp of signs, symbols and ideologies creates confusion in the minds of the poorer while the elites of society are able to maintain their colonial control. This control extends to socio-economic, political and educational fields. This theory needed the participation by the people at a more grassroots level. This was the only way to break the monopoly of the private owner who owned communication media. This theory supports the right to relevant local information, the right to answer back and the right to use the new means of communication. The theory emphasizes interaction and social action in small-scale settings of the community, or interest groups. Such things were not cared for by the free-flow of information theory (Developmental media theory or Modernization theory). The developmental media theory more or less, was governed by the authoritarian points of view. The west enforced its principles to the rest of the southern State. This benefited west's own interest. It made state dependent upon the west. The democratic participation theory on the basis of democracy where all the individuals are equal to use the resource of States. This theory wants a horzontal flow of information-a two-way flow. This theory does not like professional provisions for control. Participation and interaction are its key concepts. But mass media will not concrete the dream of this theory and the reason is that mass media has created emptiness, lowliness and consumerism in life in the contemporary free-market society. And the participation in it is not possible because media is manipulated by the politicians/parties in favour of their own interest.

The materials and messages disseminated by the western media lose their relevance because the west is not fulfilling the needs of the southern states because these things create confusion in people's minds. If Third World people accept western theories, they have to be careful about west's hegemonic designs. The western media is not aware of the norms charged, the norms of the people of Third World countries. There should be a channel, which could link both 'haves' and 'have-nots'. This is possible through only participatory theory. Through this process one could eradicate the gap in communications practice.

DEPENDENCY THEORY

The other theory is the *dependency theory,* which came into existence in the late 1960s-70s in *Latin America.* It was a consequence of the political situation in the continent, with increasing U.S. support for right - wing authoritarian governments, and partly with the realization among the educated elite that the develop mentalists approach to international communication had failed to deliver.

Without doubt, we can say that America has been able to make its position dominant in the world, in the field of business of communication. And the position of the rest of the countries is that they are left with no other but to depend upon America. According to the dependency theorists, "A necessary condition for throwing off dependent relations is to have some self sufficiency in the realm of inforniation, ideas and culture.[33]

Mowlana, a modelist, who analyzed international communication proposed a model in which two dimensions-technologies axis (hardware versus software) and communication axis (Production versus distribution) met. He defined 'technology axis in which each stage is dependent on two kinds of expertise (and property). One relates to hardware, the other to software. Production hardware includes cameras, studies, printing planets, computers, etc. Production software includes actual content items but also performance rights, management, professional norms and routine operating practices of media organizations (Know-how). Distribution hardware refers to transmitters, satellite links, transportation, home receivers, recorders, etc. Distribution software includes publicity, management, marketing and research. Both production and distribution stages are affected by (extra) as well as (intra) media variables on the production side by circumstances of ownership and the cultural and social context, and on the distribution side, by the economics of the particular media market.[34] Thus, his very idea tells us that nations are dependent on multi levels of the flow of communication. The originator of such a theory has always enjoyed a top position relegating the rest to the bottom. It is scientifically true that the top will not reach to the bottom. And the result would be that this top communication system would retain its status quo. Galtung (in Mowlana, 1985) has explained the global media pattern in term of a 'center-periphery' model, according to which the world nations can be classified as either central and dominant or periphery and dependent with a predominant flow from the former towards the latter. Certain larger, more (central) countries originate news and other media content and distribute it to their own satellites'. In general, it is the United States and the larger countries of Western Europe (France, Britain, Italy, Germany, Spain), which are more 'central' and have media satellite in tow. But China and Japan have their own satellite and the Arab world its own small galaxy. The former Soviet Union was another 'central' media power whose influence has been dissipated.[35] Galtung's opinion is that the condition of periphery is miserable and poor, the flow among them being limited. The reason is that they are out of resources of communication. The relationship among these peripheral countries is too limited; the information news/ views are not as good as at the level of the center. So, it is compulsion of the countries belonging to the periphery to depend on the center. We may say that these dependent countries are receiving information under the colonization of communication space where there *is* no choice left to them. At present, we may see this in the context of India where till today all the resources of media are governed by some groups, castes and communities. The rest of the people are dependent upon them. The likes and dislikes are dependent upon the whims of these media owners. The untouchables, downtroddens of India, are not in that condition to select the news/views. They are not left in a position to show their choice before the media giants, who don't want to circulate their resource to others. They want to share all there among their own caste community, religion and relatives. Thus, through this way, a mutual communication cannot be established. The result is disassociation, disintegration, which we see in India.

MEDIA - SOCIETY THEORY : THE MASS SOCIETY

The *Mass Society Theory* emphasizes the interdependence of institutions that exercise power and thus the integration of the media into the sources of social power and authority. It is believed that its content elements do not present the actual form of society. It only presents the interest of the power holders. About it, it is said that 'the media cannot be respected to offer a critical or alternative definition of the world, and their tendency will be to assist in the accommodation of the dependent public to their fate.[36] The media in western countries which is governed by its private owners, has created a tendency to lead to isolation of family structures. It also leads to urbanization. Such tendencies have decayed social values and people's participation has been reduced. It has established the tendency to monopoly, which breaks the ideology of democracy where every individual has a right to choose the new information. It is said that:

This theory posit that media will be controlled or run in a monopolistic way and will base an effective means of organizing people in masses as audience, consumers, markets and electrets. Mass media are usually the voice of authority, the givers of opinion and instruction and also of psychic satisfaction. The media establish a relation of dependence on the part of ordinary citizens, in respect not only of opinion but also of self-identity and consciousness. According to the most influential and articulate theorist of mass society, *C.W. Mills* (1951-1956), the mass media leads to a form of non-democratic control 'from above; with few chances to answer back.[37]

This theory does not give permission to its own criticism. The Indian mass is divided into many segments on the basis of socio-economic, political cultural, educational, caste, community, religion differences. Those who are socially, economically, politically, educationally and culturally strong have created their own level of caste, community, religion and culture. The downtrodden have their own low level. There are others who occupy neither upper nor lower position, they are in the middle. The media, under such situation, has often performed its role negatively siding with power-holders and politicians. The media can always manipulates reports in favour of the powerful neglecting the interest of the majority.

Under Marxist perspectives the media is expected to disseminate all materials in favour of the proletariat society. Marx knew it that media, when governed by the elites, will not present itself in favour of the masses. Marx states:

> The class that has the means of material production has control at the same time over the means of mental production so that, thereby, generally speaking, the ideas of those who lack the means of mental production are subject to it... in so far, therefore, as they rule as a class and determine the extent and compass of an epoch, it is self-evident that they...among other things... regulate the productions and distribution of the ideas of their age: thus their ideas are the ruling ideas of the epoch. (cited in Murdock and Golding 1,1977)[38]

Marxist theory links the ownership and the dissemination of information news/views to affirm the legitimately and the value of a classless society.

In India, in the present time, the left parties want to revolt against present ideologies of the government. Their view is that such governments do not fulfill the will of the masses. Government disseminates information in favour of their own interest, which are aimed at maintaining political status. The false need has been spread by the media, which is not a good way to improve the problems of society.

Another media society theory is based on *functionalism.* It claims to explain social practices and institution in terms of the needs of society and individuals. This theory expects that whatever the information or the content of media, it should fulfill the wish of the masses. Only such signs, symbols and metaphors will be used by the media about which the masses are familiar. This will avoid confusion and lead to the improvement of the lot of common people. This theory dapicts media as essentially self-directing and self-correcting while a political in formulation, it suits pluralist and volunteers conceptions of the fundamental mechanisms of social life and has a conservative bias to the extent that the media are likely to be seen as a means of maintaining society as it is rather than as a source of major change.[39]

It is clear from the above that this theory does not give permission to the media to function freely. It is bound to work according to the will of the people. However, without the freedom of the media, the growth and development of news/views is not possible.

This theory supposes that it is useful for social integration. Without integration there can be no agreement on goals and means and no coordinated activity. This theory not only wants to establish values in society as a whole; it also wants to reach segments within society in various ways.

The next one is *Political Economic Theory* which reveals the relation of economic and media industries and the ideological content of media. It directs research attention to the empirical analysis of the structure of ownership and control of media. It focuses on the way media-market forces operate. From this point of view, the media institution has to be considered as part of the economic system, with close links to the political system.[40] Those who are governed by the ideology of Marx analyze this theory saying that first; there has been a growth in media concentration world wide, with more and more power of ownership being concentrated in fewer hands. The tendency has shown a merger between electronic hardware and software industries (Murdock, 1550). Secondly, there has been a growing global information economy (Melody, 1990) Suxman, 1997), involving an increasing convergence between telecommunication and broad casting. Thirdly, there has been a decline both in the public sector of mass media, and in the direct public control of telecommunication (especially in Western Europe), under the banner of 'deregulation' privatization' or liberalization (Sine and Tructzschller, 1952, Mc Quail and Sine 1998). The essential prepositions of political-economic theory have not charged since earlier times but the scope for application is much wider."[41]

And due to features as above, the media has creeated gaps between the rich and the poor.

MEDIA - SOCIETY THEORY : COMMUNICATION TECHNOLOGY DETERMINISM

This theory glorifies the impact of technology, which has broken many limitations. This is only due to the effect and impact of the modern technology, which has helped to develop a sense of globalization. Technology has brought the countries of the world a great deal closer despite individual differences in religion, beliefs and other characteristics. The modern period is the result of the modern technology. 'Rosers (1986) locates turning points at the invention of writing, the beginning of printing in the 15th century, in the mid 19th century start to the telecommunication era, and the age of interactive communication beginning in 1946 with the invention of the main frame computer.[42] But these technologies are always controlled by certain power-groups which have their will and interest foremost while disseminate them. The view of H.M. Innis, the founder of *Toronto School* thinking about the media in the period after the *Second World War* attributed the characteristic features of successive ancient civilization to the prevailing dominant modes of communication, each of which will have its own 'bias' in term of societal form. Again he gives an example, the change form stone to papyrus as causing a shift from royal to priestly power. In ancient Greece, an oral tradition and a flexible alphabet favoured inventiveness and diversity and prevented the emergence of a priestly class who would have monopolied over education. The foundation and endurance of the Roman Empire was assisted by a culture of writing and documents as which legal bureaucratic institutions, capable of administrating distance provinces, could be based. Printing in its turn, challenged the bureaucratic monopoly of power and encouraged both individuals and nationalism.[43] His belief is that modern technology has the capacity to break the monopoly of traditional ruler. However, modern technology is being controlled and selfishly used by the powerful elites their own benefit. In spite of such control technology has been able to change the wide world in a global village. There is still a need to democratize technology distribution. The very concept of 'mass' implies one man in relation with the larger groups of people. The practice of mass media also implies ruler where one man's content is disseminated to others. It does not matter whether others receive it favourably or unfavourably.

Another theorist Marshal Mc Luhan says that 'the typographic extension of man brought in nationalism, industrialism and mass markets and universal literacy and education.[44] No doubt, these things have come into existence but at the implementation level countries so much of difference amongst themselves that the spirit of communication is lost. Countries of South Asia, South America for example are suffering and living under the crisis of dominant culture, which is thrown, upon them. They are unfamiliar with such cultural conditions, which only create communication gaps. At the same time, poorer countries also failed to maintain democratic norms amongst themselves.

The downfall in the value of media is due to the non-sharing of the habits among news creators and news distributors. Creators, who want to create good or important or entertaining or tradition breaking product; they are primarily concerned with improving their aesthetic techniques and with 'educating this audiences, trying to go to the fore of public demand, both in the mass media and in high culture. Distributors, on the other hand, are concerned firsts with attracting and satisfying not the largest possible audience, but the largest possible audience from those taste publics, which they define as their 'market'.[45] The conflict among them often creates turmoil in the presentable content of the media. Audiences suffer a lot for a variety of reasons. The truth is that creators and distributors want to disseminate their own taste to the mass. They do not care whether the mass will accept it or not. The compulsion of the mass is that they do not form the power group. They are not able to present their wish and will. They have to accept the content of the media, which is sent by the producers somewhat unwillingly.

There are compulsions of the profession too, as both creators and distributors have to disseminate as per the needs of the masses. 'Because the careers of creators and distributors depend on their ability to attract their contributors, they try to create products which they think will appeal to their constituents. Distributors may do this deliberately, but creators usually create cultural products that appeal to them personally, hopping that the audience will feel as they do.'[46] The gap between the media owners and the mass is created by the status of the people who control it. A specific culture often constitutes the content of the media. The present scene of the media is not very encouraging as the owners of print electronic media area concerned with maintaining their status quo, castes religion and community. They have little human sense for the poor of the rest of the society. The downtrodden people of India have remained so for long as the rulers or governments have neglected them. There is no first hand knowledge of the socio-economic, political, psychological and cultural situation of the masses as for as governing bodies are concerned. So, in spite of the rhetoric to disseminate the information according to social needs of the poor the media has signally failed to perform its duties largely because of its unfamiliarity with mass attitude. As Herbert J. Gans writes in his article *"The Politics of Culture in America: A Sociological Analysis"*-

> The most needy group in America is probably the black community until recently, Negro culture has been discouraged and even suppressed, and the black people have had to choose among films, television, fiction and art created by, for, and about the white people.[47]

The common situation among all the developing countries is that the mass media is governed by power groups and elites who are unaware of the needs of the masses. The elites have created the impression that only they can select the content right and not the downtrodden masses. The elite did not want to distribute the power and status. They want to circulate it among themselves.

'Thus, technology has no power above those who make use of it since the power to choose and distribute rests with them. The modern technology is the means of the content. The creator and distributor should want to send message and information well as allow participation of the downtrodden people.

The eastern media is by and large governed by the western theories in its mode of functioning. Indian media (Communication theory) is totally based on the Western theories of communications. P.B. Sawant, Chairman, Press Council of India, says on the position of media in his article titled *'The Press As I see It here, in vidura* Vol: 38 issue 3, July-Sept.2001 p.5.

> The rest of the society has remained almost in the same old condition with only a marginal improvement. The result therefore has been that all institution including the media continue to be in the hands of the same old dominating section, which continues to influence even today the society and the policy makers. If the press (media) is to be the mirror of the society, it will have to reflect both at the decision-making and the operational levels all sections and interests of the society and their problems, aspiration and hopes and particularly of those sections, which constitute the majority consisting of the deprived and the disadvantaged. In other words, the press media has to be rescued from the small section of the elite and made a voice of the masses that are clamoring to be recognized as equal citizens of the country. But for that, the purely commercial approach of the press has to be abandoned or an alternative/ additional

> media has to be developed. The dominating section of the press in particular has to be Indianised in its approach and content.[48]

The claim of Eastern media owners and theorists is that western theories do not give any chance to others. It has therefore maintained its dominant position reflecting the interest of other. This is no privilege but monopoly in the field of media. The other side of the coin is that those countries who claim to distribute information as per the need of the masses also exercise their implicit will to rule and maintain status quo. They too followed the principle of authoritarian, and colonization as that western masters have done in the past. The only difference between them is that the national media is governed by the national elites while the western media's interests have for more horrible consequences. The latter care only for their own economic interest.

A highly competent analysis of the western theories has been done by Prof. J.S. Yadav who writes:

> The western model of free press needs careful and critical examination in context of Asian nation. The concept of freedom and objectivity are relative and derive meaning from the context in which those are practised. The press in India and other Asian countries faces a peculiar policy dilemma. The conflict between western libertarian view of press and social responsibility of the press is becoming sharper in many Asian nations. With this comes the question of whether we are to practice 'Journalism of despair' exclusively or 'Journalism of hope' 'as well which covers both positive and negative happening in our societies. In fact, press should cover all good, bad and other news worthy of coverage. The press is ultimate analysis, along with exposing defects in public life should strive to understand the popular feelings and give them expression. More importantly as Gandhiji said, the press should strive to arousc among the people certain desirable sentiments. Thus, in Asian nations, the press in evolving its own peculiar

blend of western model and eastern concepts and requirements. The issue of development and vision of future in Asian nation are important considerations which provide peculiar flavour to the press in Asian nations.[49]

On the whole, we see that western communication theories did not fulfill the need of the poor of society, nation. The media has been charged with racism, religious fanaticism, regionalism, and desired for cultural supremacy. In Eastern mass communication theories and mostly in the context of India, racism implies casteism. Religious fanaticism, communalism and regionalism might be seen as part of Indian social life. There are other factors, which do not allow emancipation from the communication noise. These are some of the causes through which Indian communication theories are painfully passing.

The object of media is to inform, educate and entertain. This goes near the term given by Merton and Lazersfeld - *'narcotizing dysfunction'*. This implies that there is no association between the content of the media and the masses. The mass is missing from the mass media. The reason is that mass media is not willing to present its products which require the proof of masses involvement in the socio-economic development.

References

1. William L, Rivers and Wilbur *Schramm, Responsibility in Mass communication* (New York: Harper & Row Publishers, 1969), p.30.
2. *ibid,* p.30.
3. William L. Rivers and Wilbur Schramm, *Responsibility in Mass communication, p.31.*
4. William L. Rivers and Wilbur Schramm, *Responsibility in Mass communication, p.31.*
5. *Ibid.* p.31.
6. William L. Rivers and Wilbur Schramm, *Responsibility in Mass communication,* p.33.
7. *Ibid,* p.33.

8. *Ibid, p.33*
9. William L. Rivers and Wilbur Schramm, *Responsibility in Mass communication,* p.33.
10. William L. Rivers and Wilbur Schramm, *Responsibility in Mass communication,* p.35.
11. William L. Rivers and Wilbur Schramm, *Responsibility in Mass communication,* p.35.
12. William L. Rivers and Wilbur Schramm, *Responsibility in Mass communication,* p.35.
13. William L. Rivers and Wilbur Schramm, *Responsibility in Mass communication,* p.36.
14. *Ibid.* p.36.
15. William L. Rivers and Wilbur Schramm, *Responsibility in Mass communication,* p.37.
16. *Ibid.* p.39.
17. William L. Rivers and Wilbur Schrainm, *Responsibility in Mass communication,* p.39.
18. William L. Rivers and Wilbur Schramm, *Responsibility in Mass communication,* p.41.
19. William L.Rivers and Wilbur Schramm, *Responsibility in Mass communication,* p.41.
20. William S. Sahakin, Mobel Lewis Sahakian : *Idias of the Great Philosophers* (New York: Barnes and Noble Books, A division of Harper & Row Publishers, 1966), p.149.
21. William S. Sahakin, Mobel Lewis Sahakian : *Idias of the Great Philosophers,* p.149.
22. William L. Rivers and Wilbur Schramm, *Responsibility in Mass communication,* p.42.
23. *Ibid.* p.43.
24. William L. : Rivers and Wilbur Scbramm *Responsibility in Mass communication,* p.44.
25. William L. Rivers and Wilbur Schramm, *Responsibility in Mass communication,* p.46.
26. William L. : Rivers and Wilbur Schramm : *Responsibility in Mass communication,* p.48.
27. William L. : Rivers and Wilbur Schramm : *Responsibility in Mass communication,* p.50.
28. William L. Rivers and Wilbur Schramm, *Responsibility in Mass communication,* p.50.
29. *Ibid.* p.51.

30. William L. : Rivers and Wilbur Schranim : *Responsibility in Mass communication,* p.48.
31. Indira Gandhi Open University Communication Division : *Mass Media and Society* (New Delhi: 1995), p.44.
32. Wilbur Scbramm, *Mass Media and National Development; The Role of Information in the Developing Countries* (Paris Standfard University Press,1964). pp.26-27.
33. Mc Quial Denis *Mass Communication Theory* (New Delhi: Sage Publication), pp.226-27.
34. Mc Quial Denis, *Mass Communication Theory,* pp.227-28.
35. Mc Quial Denis, *Mass Communication Theory,* p.228.
36. Mc Quial Denis, *Mass Communication Theory,* p.74.
37. Mc Quial Denis, *Mass Communication Theory,* p.75.
38. Mc Quial Denis, *Mass Communication Theory, p.77.*
39. Mc Quial Denis, *Mass Communication Theory,* p.82.
40. Mc Quial Denis *Mass Communication Theory,* p.82.
41. *Ibid.* p.83.
42. Mc Quial Denis, *Mass Communication Theory,* p.85.
43. Mc Quial Denis : *Mass Communication Theory,* pp.85-86.
44. Mc Quid Denis, *Mass Communication Theory,* p.88.
45. Herbert J.Gans, *The Politics of Culture in America : A Sociological Analysis* in Mc Quial Denis (ed.) *Sociology of Mass Communiction* (Penguine Book, 1972), p.380.
46. Herbert J. Gans, *The Politics of Culture in America A Sociological Analysis* in Mc Quial Denis (ed.) *Sociology of Mass Communication,* p.230.
47. Herbert J. Gans, *The Politics of Culture in America : A Sociological Analysis* in Mc Quial Denis (ed.) *Sociology of Mass Communication,* p.385.
48. Herbert J. Gans, *The Politics of Culture in America: A Sociological Analysis* in Mc Quial Denis (ed.) *Sociology of Mass Communication,* p.230.
49. Dr. J.S.Yadav, *Is Western Model Relivent to Asia* in J.S. Yadav and Pradeep Mathur (eds.) *Issues in Mass Communication,* Vol.1 (New Delhi Kanishka Publishing, Distributors, 1998), p.137.

Right to Information Act 2005 and Mass Media : And Miles To Go ...

This act can be seen as an achievement to those who believe in the true democracy, good governance and transparency in Indian parliamatarian system. Since the history of human civilization, there has been one group who are less in number but maximum in power who think that they are born to rule over upon the 'others.' Power is 'their' legacy and no one has right to challenge it. They are the product of *manusmiriti system* where the right to colonize, exploit and destruct has been rest in them. They are used to hide the information which benefits the 'others' (orientalists) right (according to Edward Said in orientalism). They are occidentalist, capitalist (Karl Marx). They have created their own structure (structural imperialism by Galtung) in which the *Core* infringes the domain of *periphery* which is not completely but at some extent, this act has tried to step it.

Before coming on the main Act 2005, I would like to give here brief history of its journey where some politician, bureaucracy judiciary's people as well as common people of this country have contributed to give it a shape. It was 80's decade and in the corner of judiciary one murmuring sound was spreading which was located with the content corruption and scam in top class politician bureaucrats and some other institutions who were responsible to the citizen of this country. And the cause of it was 'lack of all pervading transpaney corruption and Right To Know would lead to openness, accountability and integrity as said by ex solicitor General of India Soli Sorbjee. P.B. Sawant also believed that root of this cause was the barrier to information is the single most cause responsible for corruption in society. And that is why, they all had demanded that there should be something which could solve the problem. One solution or a step was ahead by Justice Matthew in 1975 where he says that the 'people of this country have a right to know every public act, everything that is done is a public way by thier public functionaries. They are entitle to know the particulars of every public transactions in all its bearing. Their right to know, which is derived from the concept of freedom of speech and expression article 19(1)a of Indian constitution, though not absolute, is a factor which should make one wary when secrecy is claimed for transaction which can at any rate have no repercussion on public secretly. (U.P. State vs. Raj Narayan)

Next step of its crystallization was taken up by the National Front Government's Prime Minister, Honorable V.P. Singh in 1989 who once said in favour of this act that an open system of governance is an essential prerequisite for the fullest flowering of democracy. Free flow of information from the government to the people will not only create an enlightened and informed public opinion but also render those in authority accountable. In the recent past, we have witnessed many distortions in our information system. The veil of secrecy was lowered many a time not in the interest of national security, but to shield the guilty, vested interest or gross errors of judgements. Therefore this government has decided to make the 'Right to information fundamental Right..... A large area of information dissemination also relates to development programmers, their progress and their impact. This will need to be done at the Panchayat and Municipal levels, not only to encourage multi-level planning but also the common man in the villages.

It is 1996, the press Council of India and Institute of Rural Development, Hydrabad drafted the Bill was named Right To Information Bill 1996. In 1997, the Government of India appointed a working group of January 2nd and who recommended that this Bill should be named as Freedom of

Information Bill as the Right To Information has already been judicially recognized as a part of the fundamental right to free speech and expression.

P.B. Sawant then chairman of Press Council of India, drafted the Bill, keeping in view the dire need of the day and the observation made by eminent persons that in a democracy, it is people who are the masters and those utilizing public resources and exercising people power are their agents. Bill's clause 3 says that :

(a) Every citizen shall have right to information from public body,

(b) It shall be the duty of the public body to maintain all records duly catalogued, and indexed,

(c) The public body shall be under a duty to make available to the person requesting information, as it is under an obligation to obtain and furnise and shall not withhold any information or limit its availability to the public except the information specified in clause (4) and

(d) All individual whether citizen or not, shall have the right to such information that affects their life and liberty.

Mass movement was started and they demanded Right To Information. A mass based organization which called Mazdoor Kisan Shakti Sangathan (MKSS) took initiative to lead the people in very backward region of Rajasthan Bhim Tehsil to assert their right to information and they demanded copies of bills and vouchers and name of persons who have been paid wages mentioned in muster rolls-on the construction of public school and hospitals and so on.

Any how, finally Right To Information Act came in 2005. Areas were specified from where the citizen of this union can know whats going on. But as we know that no right can be absolute, the chance of improvement is always there. Here I would like to quote one paragraph which would clear its meaning.

"An Act provide for setting out the practical regime of right to information for citizens to secure *access to information under the control of public authorities, in order to promote transparency and accountability in the working of every public authority,* the constitution of a Central Information Commission and State Information Commission and for a matters connected therewith or incidental threto."

Again its is written that the "information' means and material in any form, including records, documents, memos, e-mail, opinions, advices, press releases, circulars, orders, begbooks, contracts, reports, papers, samples, models, daté material held in any electronic form and information relating to any private body which can be accessed by a public authority under only other law for the time being in force.

(From the Gazette page 2-3)

Alongwith it some areas are also mentioned from where we (the citizen of this union) cannot get information on which are mentioned below

(a) Information, disclosure of which would prejudicially affect the sovereignty and integrity of India, the security, strategic, scientific or economic interests of the State, relation with foreign State or lead to incitement of an offence.

(b) Information which has been expressly forbidden to be published by any court law or tribunal or the disclosure of which may constitute contempt of court.

(c) Information, the disclosure of which would cause a breach of privilege of parliament or the state legislature.

(d) Information including commercial confidence, trade secrets or intellectual property, the disclosure of which would harm the competitive position of a third party, unless the competent authority to satisfied that larger public interest warrants the disclosure of such information.

(e) Information available to a person in his fiduciary relationship, unless the competent authority is satisfied that the larger public interests warrants the disclosure of such information.

(f) Information received in confidence from foreign government.

(g) Information the disclosure of which would endanger the life or physical safety of any person or identify the source of information or assistance given in confidence for law enforcement or security purposes.

(h) Information which would impede the process of investigation or apprehension or prosecution of offenders.

(i) Cabinet papers including records distribution of the council of Ministers, Secretaries and other officers.

And official secrets Act, 1923's rules and some others are too.

R.T.I. AND MASS MEDIA

Mass media also get a chance to utilize the benefits of then law and that's results can be seen after knowing the recent events which were covered by it. Some names are here given like (C W G Scam. New Delhi, Adarsh Society Scam Maharstra Vedanta in Orissa, 2G spectrum and some others are revealed with the help of this act where it was shown that law the money of common people is misused by the incurred cancer of Indian society. But we should not forget that modern media in India is also run by the capitalists who too do not want to spread those information which could make the common. People rich for that they are suffering from countries.

But only the periphery's people are caught and captured by the mass media where as 'core' is concerned till date it is enjoying its power. In 2G spectrum alliance party's minister has to resign. Are congress party members not corrupt? Yes they are but like Natwar Singh and others who were challenging the legacy .... of family of power, result is before you. This core has created *fubbe society* where others are not allowed to inter at that place where the 'core' is and more or less it can be seen in every institute of Indian society. Nira Radia case has recently revealed that how she was lobbying and giving benefits to the 'choosen few' or 'our' (Edward Said). After this event, media is also exposed and 'paid content', manipulation of information to give benefits to the politician bureaucrats and judiciary's people or the authority cannot be hidden. It is proved where as R.T.I. is concerned it is also not reaching at that place where it should because of the lock of 'National character' which was dramed by our for fathers saints, faker and social reformers. Really, till date Gandhi is killed non-violence is murdered.

RESULT OF R.T.I. ACT

Some R.T.I. activists who have last their lives must not be forgotten because it shows the character of this country which claims it is civilized and cultured where some people who do not want to break the legacy of manusmirity and occidental mind set. Some names are here who have become immortal, because they wanted to break thousand years old the their legacy. Amit Jethw (35) July 20, 2010 Gujarat, Datta Patil (47) May 22, 2010 Maharastra. Setis Shetty (39) January 2010 Pune, Vitthal Gite (39) April 21, 210 Maharastra , Shasidhar Mishra Barauni Bihar, Feb. 2010, Manju Nath S. U.P. 2000 Lakhimpuri Khird, Satendra Dubey Nov. 2003 Bihar, Venkatesh April 2010 Bangalore and Sola Raja Rao (30) Andra Pradesh and some other are too who are not covered. Some are living but living a Life-in-Death. (T.S. Eliot) Really this Act is beginning not and end, And miles to go ....

